FAR COUNTRY

by

John F. Deane

⌐DEDALUS

The Dedalus Press
24 The Heath
Cypress Downs
Dublin 6W
Ireland

"Icarus" series number one, first October 1992
Edition limited to 350 copies

i.m. Daniel Patrick Deane (1908 - 1990)

ISBN 1 873790 17 1

Cover drawing, "Fisherman" by John Behan.

Printed in Ireland

contents

Out on the current a black hag swam,
bright eye, and head erect; again and again it dived
down on its own blackness, exploratory, in hope ...

ON ANOTHER SHORE

The worn-out Otherthing
rigid on its slab, the fluids
stagnant;
dressed up and parcelled – the Offence;

someone had set a plastic rose
upon the chest,
and we, attendants,
faces unmasked by grief,

murmured our studied words;
he is not dead, but sleeping,
he is not here,
he has stepped out on another shore

beautiful beyond belief;
and we have crept back out
into weakened sunshine,
knowing our possibilities

diminished.

THE CURRENT

The man was standing, up to his thighs in slip-water,
spinning; concentrated, eager, his hands
exact with rod and water-coloured gut;

I was digging in sand behind him, safe
from the wildering rush of the current;
periwinkles breathed small bubbles in the pools

and barnacles clung to the rough rock surfaces;
I hammered on their backs with stones
and watched the water-blood

seep from the shattered shells;
sometimes the shoals of mackerel broke
into the shallows near him, famished,

frenzied through the living mercury of eels;
I pictured them, out there, the shoals,
streaming through the cold, inhuman forests

of the underworld, aghast, and wraithlike;
the man was making his way homewards over rocks,
mackerel strung by their gills on twine,

fish-scales, fish-blood, ghosting his clothes
and I beside him, quietened,
clinging to his rough, red hands, for hold.

FERRY

The waves between the islands
were dark green walls
rising against us;

I cried aloud with the thrill of it,
the throbbing vessel hoisted high
and held — while we watched a moment

towards our fall, that
lurching helplessness down down down;
his face was bright with merriment, his glasses

wet from sea-spray;
sea-birds, auk and guillemot and shearwater
insolent, in their element, about us;

too soon we had reached harbour, the boat
juddering clouds of silt through the clear water,
dull thud of wooden taffrail against concrete;

I grew nervous then of his big body
stepping out between gunwale and pier,
my small hand stretched up uselessly to help;

shorefall, the pale road upwards,
distances, and waves between the islands
rising again between us.

WHEEL

Northwards the rain
brushes grey over the world; westwards
distance, black impasto clouds;
in a blunt Ford Prefect

smelling of oiled upholstery, tobacco, must,
I hold the big, moulded, driving wheel;
around us the island sandybanks,
the obstacles are sheep,

streams, and hare-track culverts;
the future is there, beyond the dashboard,
out over the bonnet, a huge,
a virgin canvas. Father,

straight-backed, fleshed out with tenderness,
holds my fingers on the wheel;
noon, and stillness, the first day;
he is gazing out the rear window

over sand-dunes, an ochre strand, the sea,
the skin of his face
finger-applied out of limed clay;
God's image, in waistcoat

and grey collarless shirt,
the white stud dangling.
Still life. Already, far out,
wings of the black hag fold over the current.

SCYTHE

He has been moving
on the widening circumference
of a circle of his own making;

eye bright, back straight, and head erect;
his shirt-sleeves folded, sweat on his flesh,
intoxicating clover-pollen, daisy-dust,

rising to him, and the high grass –
in breathless ballet – falling at his feet;
he has achieved a rhythm

that takes him from us for a while,
his soul a hub of quietness,
his body melting into the almost perfect

elliptical orbitting of the world;
soon he will flop down tiredly amongst us,
his thoughts, as after sex, moving

on the heroes of myth and literature
while the grass at the centre of his circle
has begun, imperceptibly, to green.

ISLANDMAN

1.

As in a book of origins, he comes
striding down a long, cleft valley,
cartridge-belts ebullient across his chest,
the rifle riding gently on his arm;
mountains lift their names about him –
Bunowna, Croghaun, Bunnafreva, Keem;

clouds rip themselves against high craglands;
I, cowering somewhere in his potency,
hear the distant pounding of the ocean,
the sky is filled with all the space
between Achill and America;
up in the hills, the mountain goats run free;

the soft peat floor is treacherous,
eager, like time, to take its prey
and hold it in its juices; he has climbed
cliff-slopes salted with gull-droppings,
and paused by the ghosts of old stone boleys;
I whisper my name into the bowl of time –

his head jerks upwards, and he frowns.

2.

The long hay-loft was low
and raftered like the island chapel;
among the undersides of slates,
snow-falls of ageing plaster, star-holes,
he taught me how to climb from beam to beam,
my feet never touching the ground;

he showed me how to fall, cat-soft,
into mothering hay, and I never dreamed
the rough stone floor of the future;
once I dressed up to look like him,
strutting with waders, cartridge-belts and rifle;
now he is in my words, my diffidence,

he has been dressing himself again in my flesh.

3.

Island. Still point
in a turbulent sea. A man, among others,
islanded, unquiet, pacing the shore
or stalking winter geese through a chill dusk;
old Sarah Coyne, sidling and grinning,
comes showing her withered arm;

and there, cracked Willie Slate
pissing on the road before the tourists;
anything, to keep the prowler from the heart;
war reports on the wireless, and de Valera
pelted with stones at Achill Sound.
It is easy to say "I love you" to the dead,

the words are a hard, packed ball
beaten and beaten against a high, blank wall;
but he whispers his name to me still, comes
striding down a long, cleft valley,
mountains lifting their names about him –
Bunowna, Croghaun, Bunnafreva, Keem.

FUGITIVE

Old man, in corded, ripe-plum dressing-gown,
sitting out, and silent; beyond high windows
are blood-bright tulips, funerary
wind-blown daffodils. Love comes

blundering about him; he
holds himself apart, intent upon his going,
abandons me mid-season, my words
all, like petals, falling about my feet.

THE CIRCLE

1

Darkness. Wind about the house brushing against our walls. I could sense, through shut eyelids, the lighter shade of curtains between the blacknesses within and those without.

In the new suburbs there are no trees to soften the winds and to give them names. We huddle among painted bricks and rafters, alarms primed to scream, hoping the foliage will grow, quickly, round us.

I folded my body up under the electric blanket. The wind, not animal, tore clematis from the garden walls, knocked down the sweet, red-painted, bird-tables. After a time, I slept.

Old man naked. Laid on a farmhouse kitchen table, on thick, scrubbed timbers. His long body the colour of sour cream. His hands along the timbers, raw, at his sides. The chest-hair thick, grey-white. The face, inscrutable, as always. Vague figures shifting round him, presences, unnamed. I see the wild and wintering grey-lag, shot.

Again. I stand above. Below, a patch of earth. Black clay. Cleared ground. Huddled at a distance, in heavy coats, halt, people. Indistinct, but shocked. Old man naked. The body whiter than known white. Lying at the edge of the earth, at an angle. Knees drawn up, birthing, hands raised above the head, pleading innocence. I see the wild and wintering grey-lag, shot. Soon, I wake.

3

He was sitting at the foot of a bed, on a high, hospital chair. I noticed the steel end of the bed, the steel handle, like the cranking-handle of an old Ford Prefect. The sheets rigid with white, the counterpane, light-blue, smoothed out. He was sitting perfectly still, hands on his lap, head lowered. The pink, bare skull, the few white hairs on the nape of the neck. The collar of his dressing-gown had one side folded in on itself. Small tufts of hair in his ear.

Old man. Exposed to the wildering rush of the current.

He was turned at an angle from me, motionless. And knowing. He had taken himself already a great distance from the ward. I was reluctant to bring him back. Through the wide, hospital window, the rough sea-shore of rooftops. I touched him on the shoulder. He turned his face towards me, gathering himself back out of his preparations. And looked. My own, tense face, staring, unseeing, up at me. Frightened. Tear-full. The hands, reaching upwards, for hold.

FAR COUNTRY

1.

He told us Pushkin, Tolstoy, Gogol;
we were Tatar and Cossack, I was Taras Bulba

leading moustachioed hordes over drain and árdán,
my short pants wide as the Black Sea,

Bunnacurry the Ukraine
and Stoney River the Dnieper.

2.

I watched him pacing the stone flags of the kitchen floor,
hands in his pockets, eyes cast down;
he was ranging across the steppes of his imagination,

his fair-country, the immensity of his white land,
bright meadow, ballroom, serf,
the poet, duelling, at dawn,

standing in a net of leaf-shadow,
the tallow candle in its copper candlestick
so tragically pinched out.

3.

For years he worked at a deal table
cumbered with files and documents
while a harassed people, rough-handed, old,
came to him with forms;

sometimes he held a match to a stub of wax
and watched its one big drop of blood
fall heavily. His eyes were glazed with dust,
his long legs curled.

4.

Together we stepped down onto the tarmac,
he was silent, pleading,

home at last, reach, toe-tip, hold
like Daedalus after his hazardous flight;

old now, and slow, he was entering through the sliding
glass doors of his dream,

suffering the long
low customs hall, passport control,

questioned for currency, for proof
he was who he thought he was and no other.

5.

By day we were Intourists, on an Intourist bus,
viewing mechanical glories of the Revolution.
We queued for hours to see the saint,
shambling, like convicts, between rows of guards;

stepped down, out of the sun, into a crypt,
where Lenin lies, uncorrupted, under glass,
plans for the reconstruction of the world
frozen in his head; a dead man's bedroom

but you cannot touch the folded hands
or put your lips to the alabaster brow.
Father was silent, pleading; at night I heard him
turn in his bed, utter small, hurt, animal cries.

6.

At last, at dawn, in the airport terminal,
I saw him sitting, radiant,

under the chandeliers of Russian words,
speaking with an old official at a desk

who dropped wax blood onto yellow forms;
they spoke of weather, traffic, snow,

of Pushkin, Tolstoy, Gogol,
the summer and winter palaces

that were still standing
bright as birthday cakes in their fair country.